What Others Say About Doug Giles

"I think Doug Giles brings a sharp, humorous, bold and captivating style to ministry that strikes a chord with young people."

– Dr. R.C. Sproul

"There is NO way to describe Doug Giles adequately, so I won't even try. Suffice it to say there is NO ONE like him and I'm grateful for him!"

– Eric Metaxas

"Doug Giles speaks the truth ... he's a societal watchdog ... a funny bastard."

– Ted Nugent

"Doug Giles is a good man, and his bambinas are fearless. His girls Hannah and Regis Giles are indefatigable. I admire the Giles clan from afar."

– Dennis Miller

"Doug Giles must be some kind of a great guy if CNN wants to impugn him."

– Rush Limbaugh

Recommendations for *The Art of Joe*

"Doug Giles' compendium of Joe Biden's political savvy is both orthoscopic and prophetic. If you don't understand this, then it's your fault and I have neither the time nor the crayons to explain it to you." (Producer of the smash hit, The Yellow River, Dr. I.P. Freely)

"Prescient!" (From the producer of the blockbuster film, Under the Grandstands, Seymour Hiney)

"Doug Giles has done yeoman's work with his compilation and communication of Biden's weltanschauung. This is an instant classic!" (Facebook post from the screenwriter of Deep in Debt, Mr. Owen A. Lott)

"Move over Frederic Bastiat" (Paul Bearer, host of the podcast, Depressing Jobs)

"Real. Raw. Righteous. Relevant. Giles has truly shown the light on Biden's understanding of our complicated political landscape and his ideas for moving our country forward. Bravo!" (Harry Chin, author of the bestselling book on foreign policy, The Hairy Chinaman)

"A great book. This should be required reading for all school children. Thank you, Mr. Giles." (Tweet from D. I. Aria)

"All I can say is, Qualem muleirculam!" (Jacques Strappe, founder of the NGO, Supporting Athletes)

"Easy to read. I read it twice in one sitting."(Darren Dabarne, Executive producer, Where Have All The Animals Gone?)

Published by White Feather Press.
(www.whitefeatherpress.com)

ISBN 978-1-61808-205-3

Printed in the United States of America

Cover design by David Bugnon and mobopolis.com

The Art of Joe

狗屁

The Political Brilliance of President Biden

By Doug Giles

Dedication

Dear Biden Voters.

I have put my heart and soul into this book and I
am dedicating it, with love, to you.

Herewith is "why" one should respect and re-
elect, Joe Biden.

Tolle Lege,
Doug Giles
Caracas, Venezuela
August, 2021

Table of Contents

Introduction

Joe Biden has shaken the United States to its core with his bold new vision and leadership for America! Finally, in this thoroughly researched tome, we have gathered what Giles is calling, 'The Biden Doctrine.'

No doubt, this document will give fans and foes a deep look inside of Biden's political philosophy and how it frames his leviculus policy positions.

The Art of Joe: The Political Brilliance of President Biden is an essential document for those who take our political discourse very, very, very seriously. We recommend the reader buy five extra copies to pass out to young college students who they know and love. It's that important.

Skip Coryell
President, White Feather Press

chapter 1. Afghanistan

chapter 2. Economics

chapter 3. The Plague and Stuff

chapter 4. Immigration

chapter 5. National Security

chapter 6. God

chapter 7. Corn Pop

Chapter 8. Health Care

chapter 9. Planes, Trains and Automobiles

chapter 10. Edumication

chapter 11. The Constitution

chapter 12. Abortion

chapter 13. Racism, Riots and Police Reform

chapter 14. Climate change

chapter 15. The 2nd Amendment

Chapter 16. The #MeToo Movement

chapter 17. why Karl Marx was Right

chapter 18. The Thing

chapter 19. The Devil Incarnate

Epilogue: Notable Quotable Joe

One of my favorite things to do, as an author and a public speaker, is to garner great quotes from famous folks and parlay them upon my crowd for their edification, education and amusement.

I always search for epic quotes that are universally significant, brilliant, direct and succinct. I believe, and history will prove me right, that Joe Biden's maxims and idioms; his crafty turn of phrases and mastery of the English language will ensconce him, in perpetuity, as one of the world's most notable quotable individuals.

The following Biden quotes, antidotes and short stories should survive for years; nay, centuries, because they strike a divine chord in the hearts of those who aspire to excellence in all things.

I believe Biden will share space with the great orators such as Demosthenes, Chrysostom, St. Augustine, Socrates, Plato, Lincoln, Keats, Churchill, Emerson, Britney Spears and Beavis & Butthead.

Enjoy the following and commit them to memory for, you too, could be a great philosophizing, raconteur or whatever, like Joe.

Biden on the Taliban

July 8: "The likelihood there's going to be the Taliban overrunning everything and owning the whole country is highly unlikely... it is not inevitable."

August 18: "The idea that somehow, there's a way to have gotten out without chaos ensuing, I don't know how that happens."

Biden on the Afghan Army

July 8: "I trust the capacity of the Afghan military, who more competent [than the Taliban] in terms of conducting war."

August 18: "When you saw the significant collapse of the Afghan troops we had trained, that was -- you know I'm not -- that's what happened."

Biden on the Evacuation of the American Embassy in Kabul

July 8: "There's going to be no circumstance when you're going to see people being lifted off the roof of an embassy. It's not at all comparable [with Saigon]."

Biden on the Afghan Government

July 8: "The Afghan leadership has the capacity to sustain the government in place."

August 18: "You had the government of Afghanistan, the leader of that government, get in a plane and taking off and going to another country."

Biden on Afghan Translators

July 8: "We can guarantee their safety."

August 18: "The Taliban control the area around Kabul airport and have shot and beaten crowds of people trying to get through for evacuation."

Biden On Corn Pop

"I learned ... I learned a lot. And I learned that ... uh ... it makes a difference. This was the diving board area and I was one of the guards and they weren't allowed. It was a three meter board and you fell off sideways you landed on the damn, the darn, cement over there."

"Corn Pop was a bad dude and he ran a bunch of bad boys. And I did, yeah he and back in those days, the shot things have changed. One of the things you had to use if you used pomade in your hair you had to wear a bathing cap. And so he was up on the board. Wasn't listening. I said, "Hey Esther! You off the board or I'll come up and drag you off." Well ... he came off and he said, "I'll meet you outside my car." This was mostly, these were all public housing behind it. My car there was a gate out here I parked my car outside the gate and I he said, "I'll be waiting for you." He was waiting for three guys in straight razors. Not a joke."

"There was a guy named Bill Wright Mouse. The only white guy and he did all the pools. He was the mechanic and I said, "What am I going to do?" He said, "Come down here in the basement where mechanics where where all the pool filter is. You know, the chain used to be a chain that went across the deep end and he cut off a six foot length of chain he fold up he said, "You walk out with that chain and you walk to the car and say, "You may cut me man, but i'm going to wrap this chain around your head."

I said, "You kidding me?" He said, "No, if you don't don't come back" and he was right."

"So I walked out with the chain and I walked up to my car and they had those days used to remember the straight razors? Bang them on the curb. Get them rusty. Put them in a rain barrel. Get them rusty. And I looked at them, but I was smart, then I said, first of all, I said, "When I tell you get off the board, you get off the board and I'll kick you out again but I shouldn't have called you Esther Williams. I apologize for that. I apologize but I know that apology is going to work." He said, "You apologize to me?" I said, "I apologize for that, not for throwing you out, but I apologize for what I said." He said, "Okay." Closed the straight razor and my heart began to beat again."

Biden on *The Declaration of Independence*

"We hold these truths to be self-evident that all men and women created by ... the go ... you know ... the you know ... the thing."

Biden on COVID

COVID has taken this year just since the outbreak has taken more than 100 years. Look, here's the lives it's just, it's when you think about it.

Biden on Who Knows?

"You know the rapidly rising ... uh ... um ... uh, in with ... uh ... with ... uh, I don't know ... uh."

Biden on His "Dartmouth" Speech

"I just spoke at a at Dartmouth on healthcare at the medical school or, not I guess. I wasn't actually on the campus but people from the medical school right there. I want to be clear. I'm not going nuts. I'm not sure whether it's a medical school or where the hell I spoke but it's on the campus."

Biden on the "Cancer Moon Shot'

"I propose, and i'm going to digress slightly, like here we we're in a situation I president asked me to head up a cancer moon shot."

Biden on International Affairs

"Guatemala, El Salvador and and it would take us to go in and say, in Honduras and say, "look!"

Biden Confronts Putin

"I took on ... uh ... Putin. In terms of ... uh ... Iraq, I mean excuse me, in terms of ... uh ... um ... what was going on in Ukraine?"

Biden on Hard Work

"We can't afford it by just eliminating beginning to treat treat work, reward work, as much as well."

Biden Describes His Legs

"I get hot. I got a lot of, I got hairy legs that turn that that that that that turn ... uh ... blonde in the sun and the kids used to come up and reach in the pool and rubbed my leg down so it was straight and then watch the hair come back up again."

Biden on Self Defense

"If you want to protect yourself get a double barrel shotgun. Have the shells a 12 gauge shotgun."

Biden on Children

"I learned about roaches. I learned about kids jumping on my lap and I've loved kids jumping on my lap."

Biden vs. Trump

"I said, if we were in high school, I'd take him behind the gym and beat the hell out of him."

Biden calls out Trump

"Trump was out there tweeting again this morning. I called him President Tweedy."

More Criticism of Trump

"Well, Trump is protruding, pursuing, a damage in an erratic trade war. Without any strategy, by the way."

Even More Trump Critiques

"He doesn't want to shed light, he wants to generate heat. And he's stroking violence in our cities."

Biden on His Mental Health

"Mental filth. My physical, as well as my Mental fitness."

Biden on Dancing Girls

"I want to see these terrible young ladies. I want to see them dancing when they're four years older too."

Biden vs. Trump Debates

"I'm looking forward to this, man. You walk behind me in a debate? Come here man."

Biden and the Climate Crisis

"We can't rebuild our economy and meet this climate crisis exacerbating the need for example firms up environmental justice. Sorry, that's a bug."

Biden on Partnerships

"It far more durable, reliable and powerful and partnerships built on cohesion, excuse me, coercion."

Biden on Department Stores

"If you were a quartermaster, you can sure in health ... take care of running a ... you know ... department store ... uh ... thing. You know... where ... and the second floor of the ladies department or, whatever, you know what I mean."

"I have no clue what he's talking about here."

"And what makes his wild claims and hopes he now hopes we don't notice what he said. I won't remember

and when he does follow through or doesn't do would follow through the exact opposite."

Biden on Spaghetti

"So you go ahead and you stack spaghetti sauce at a store and a supermarket, you control the guy or the woman, who runs, the run, brings out the carts on on on a forklift. What happened?

Biden on China

"The way Trump, the way China will respond, is when we gather the rest of the world, that in fact invades, and and free in ... in ... in ... open trade and making sure that we're in a position that the world ... uh ... that ... that we deal with, who, the right way. That, then in fact, that's when things began to change."

Biden's Plan

"I ... uh ... you know ... I ... I looked at it anyway. I, that's what I think my plan, I know what my plan does."

Biden on God only Knows

"I mean, no ... no ... but I mean, think, about I mean it's not, about I know, you're supporting by saying booing but look here's the deal."

Biden and his Nurse

"I had a nurse at, nurses at, Walter Reed Hospital who would bend down and whisper in my ear and go home and get me pillows. They would make sure they'd actually, probably nothing, ever taught in ...

*uh ... you can't do it in the covered time but they'd
actually breathe in my nostrils. To make me move. To
get get me moving."*

Biden on Election Integrity

*"We can do about it is be prepared. We have a whole
group of lawyers who are going out to every polling
every ... uh .... voter registration physician in the
states. The secretaries of state making sure that they
in fact have a game plan as to how they're going to
allow the voting take place."*

COVID'S Death Toll

*"200 million people have died probably by the time I
finish this talk."*

Biden's Time in the Senate

*"That's why i made it a priority my entire career to
work closely with you from the time I got to the senate
180 years ago."*

Biden's Icebreaker

*"You know where you were anyway, welcome to the
nation's Constitution Center. I had the great privilege
of being the guest leader this outfit for a year. It's an
appropriate place to make the speech I'm about to
make."*

Biden Anticipates Debating Trump

*"I ... I ... know you're trying to goad me but I mean
I'm so forward-looking to have an opportunity to sit
with the president or stand with the president and
debates."*

Biden on his Mental Health.

"I want to be clear I'm not going nuts."

Biden on Truth

"We choose truth over facts."

Biden on Barack

"One legend stands ready to deliver change we desperately need. A man I'm proud to call my friend. A man who will be the next president of the United States. Barack America!"

Biden on Obama Care

"This is a big fucking deal."

Biden on being Straightforward

"We can speak out and be more straightforward. I'm not gonna be a muon. I ... I ... I .... I ... I ... got something new. I gotta go do ... boom ... boom ... boom."

Biden on Energy

"That saves billions of gallons of gasoline. I mean billions of two point, I think. It's two point three billion dollars. Worth of assuming, five hundred billion dollars in savings and two point something billion metric tons of co2 going in the air."

Biden on Tax Loopholes

"Well, folks. I eliminate one tax loophole out of a trillion six hundred billion worth for a trillion four hundred billion worth out of a billion four hundred million. I submit trillion four hundred billion dollars. It's hard even saying it so much and by the way. It's cost a lot of money. It cost about seven hundred forty million billion dollars over ten years. Billion dollars over ten years."

Biden on Obama

"Now is the time to heed the timeless advice from Teddy Roosevelt: "Speak softly and carry a big stick." I promise you, the president (Obama) has that big stick. I promise you."

Biden Confronts Townhall Attendee

"I was a Democratic caucus at Mendel caucus. No you have it. You're a lying, dog face, pony-soldiers. You said you are but yeah now you got to be honest. I'm gonna be honest with you."

Biden on Black Kids

"We have this notion that somehow, if you're poor you cannot do it. Poor kids are just as bright and just as talented as white kids, wealthy kids, black kids."

Bibliography

About the Author

Doug earned his Bachelor of Fine Arts degree from Texas Tech University and his certificates in both Theological and Biblical Studies from Knox Theological Seminary (Dr. D. James Kennedy, Chancellor). Giles was fortunate to have Dr. R.C. Sproul as an instructor for many classes.

Doug Giles is the host of ClashRadio.com, the co-founder and co-host of the Warriors & Wildmen podcast (660K downloads) and the man behind ClashDaily.com. In addition to driving Clash-Daily.com (260M+ page views), Giles is the author of several #1 Amazon bestsellers including his most recent book, If Masculinity Is "Toxic", Call Jesus Radioactive.

Doug is also an artist and a filmmaker and his online gallery can be seen at DougGiles.Art. His first film, Biblical Badasses: A Raw Look at Christianity and Art, is available via DougGiles.Art.

Doug's writings have appeared on several other print and online news sources, including Townhall.com, The WashingtonTimes, The Daily Caller, Fox Nation, Human Events, USA Today, The Wall Street Journal, The Washington Examiner,American Hunter Magazine, and ABC News.

Giles and his wife Margaret have two daughters, Hannah and Regis. Hannah devastated ACORN with her 2009 nation-shaking undercover videos and she currently stars in the explosive 2018 Tribeca Documentary, Acorn and The Firestorm.

Regis has been featured in Elle, American Hunter, and Variety magazines. Regis is also the author of a powerful new book titled, How Not To Be A #Me-Too Victim, But A #WarriorChick.

Regis and Hannah are both black belts in Gracie/Valente Jiu-Jitsu.

Speaking Engagements

Doug Giles speaks to college, business, community, church, advocacy and men's groups throughout the United States and internationally. His expertise includes issues of Christianity and culture, masculinity vs. wussification, God and government, big game hunting and fishing, raising righteous kids in a rank culture, the Second Amendment, personal empowerment, and social change. To invite Doug to speak at your next event, log on to DougGiles. org and fill out the invitation request.

Accolades for Giles include ...

– Giles was recognized as one of "The 50 Best Conservative Columnists Of 2015"

– Giles was recognized as one of "The 50 Best Conservative Columnists Of 2014"

– Giles was recognized as one of "The 50 Best Conservative Columnists Of 2013"

– ClashDaily.com was recognized as one of "The 100 Most Popular Conservative Websites For 2013 and 2020"

– Doug was noted as "Hot Conservative New Media Superman" By Politichicks

Between 2002 – 2006, Doug's 3-minute daily commentary in Miami received seven Silver Microphone Awards and two Communicator Awards.

What others say about Doug Giles

For a generation, at least, Western Society has been leveling its ideological guns on men -- that is on males, "maleness". For a good chunk of that stretch, Doug Giles -- author, hunter, commentator, broadcaster -- has taken up the cause of his fellow "dudes". His latest salvo in this desperately needed pro-XY chromosome crusade is If Masculinity Is 'Toxic', Call Jesus Radioactive. Delivered in the lively, inimitable style those familiar with Doug have come to recognize, the book confronts modern-day misandry, head on. The significance of dads, husbands, sons, brothers -- men! -- has become one of the gasping and endangered themes of our effeminized, gender-addled era. With the release of this newest tome, Doug aims to pump some life back into that foundational truth. If Masculinity Is 'Toxic', Call Jesus Radioactive tracks through the Gospel of Matthew -- a winning, easy-to-follow format -- highlighting how Jesus demonstrates what God expects of men. For all that, the book goes a long way toward sketching much of what the Creator envisions for every person -- so the ladies will benefit from perusing these pages as well.

Steve Pauwels
Editor-In-Chief, DailySurge.com

"Giles aims his arrows at the pusillanimous pastors who have bred a generation of mamby pamby Christian men who cower before the wicked. Giles challenges 'Rise up O men of God!'"

- Steven Hotze, MD
Hotze Health & Wellness Center

Doug's podcast can be seen and heard at

ClashRadio.com.

Books by Doug Giles

If Masculinity is 'Toxic' Call Jesus Radioactive

Would Jesus Vote For Trump?

Rules For Radical Christians: 10 Biblical Disciplines for Influential Believers

Pussification: The Effeminization Of The American Male

Raising Righteous And Rowdy Girls

Raising Boys Feminists Will Hate

Rise, Kill and Eat: A Theology of Hunting From Genesis to Revelation.

If You're Going Through Hell, Keep Going

My Grandpa is a Patriotic Badass

A Coloring Book for College Cry Babies

Sandy Hook Massacre: When Seconds Count, Police Are Minutes Away

The Bulldog Attitude: Get It or … Get Left Behind

A Time To Clash

10 Habits of Decidedly Defective People: The Successful Loser's Guide to Life

Political Twerps, Cultural Jerks, Church Quirks

Biblical Badasses: The Women

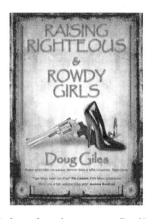

It has been said that daughters are God's revenge on fathers for the kind of men they were when they were young. Some would say that both Doug Giles and I, given our infamous pasts, are charter members of that club. However, Doug and I know that his two wonderful daughters and my equally wonderful daughter and two granddaughters are truly God's fantastic gift. With the wisdom of hindsight and experience Doug has written the ultimate manual for dads on raising righteous and rowdy daughters who will go out into the world well prepared- morally, physically, intellectually and with joyful hearts- to be indomitable and mighty lionesses in our cultural jungle. Through every raucous and no-holds-barred page, Doug, the incomparable Dad Drill Sergeant, puts mere men through the paces to join the ranks of the few, the proud, and the successful fathers of super daughters. The proof of Doug Giles' gold-plated credentials are Hannah and Regis Giles- two of the most fantastic, great hearted and accomplished young ladies I have ever known. This is THE BOOK that I will be giving the father of my two precious five and three year old granddaughters. Tiger Mom meet Lion Dad!

— Pat Caddell

Former Fox News Contributor —

Made in the USA
Coppell, TX
05 September 2021